Efflorescence

Kelsey Villeret

Legacy Book Press LLC
Camanche, Iowa

Copyright © 2021 Kelsey Villeret

Cover design by Kaitlea Toohey,
kaitleatoohey.com

Cover art by Kelsey Villeret

Cover art texture by Marjan Blan

All rights reserved. No part of this book may be used or reproduced by any means, graphic, electronic, or mechanical, including photocopying, recording, taping or by any information storage retrieval system without the written permission of the publisher except in the case of brief quotations embodied in critical articles and reviews.

ISBN: 978-1-7347986-7-8
Library of Congress Number: 1-10088701341

To my mother,
who will come to find out that I swear a lot more than she thinks.

TABLE OF CONTENTS

ACKNOWLEDGEMENTS 5
FLOWERING OUT 7
SOMEONE TO BLAME... 8
SAYING GOODBYE 9
REASSURANCE 11
PAST TENSE... 13
THAT MORNING WAS DIFFERENT 14
WHILE I WAS SAT AT THE BOTTOM OF THE SWIMMING POOL
 16
WISH LIST 17
VICTORIAN DEATH PHOTOGRAPHY 18
TAKE A PICTURE 19
SELFISH... 20
POISON 21
HOLDING HOME 22
IT'S A PROCESS 23
FAMILIAR 24
SUPPLY AND DEMAND 26
RUSSIAN NESTING DOLLS 27
VOLUNTEER WORK... 30
BEDTIME PRAYER... 31
I AM THE GIRL WITH THE ROSE TATTOO 32
NEW ADDICTIONS.. 34
ALL THE SEASONS OF YOU 35
CHEESY DOMESTIC FANTASIES.................................. 37
HER TREK 38

EYES LIKE THE OCEAN	39
BANDAIDS	41
LIGHTHOUSE	42
A DIFFERENT KIND OF MAGIC	43
GOOD MORNING	45
PARTY'S OVER	46
BEING HUMAN	48
WILD NIGHTS	49
I'M STILL TRYING	50
PAPERCUTS	51
OR MAYBE I JUST THINK TOO MUCH	52
THE DEATH OF VENUS	53
APRIL	55
EXCERPT FROM THE ONLY LOVE LETTER MY FATHER EVER WROTE	57
PATIENCE IS A VIRTUE	58
TIRED	61
I TOLD THE BEETLE	62
HANDS	64
REMEMBER ME	66
OR MAYBE HE'S STILL GONE	67
GROW WITH ME	69
OR AM I BEING GREEDY	70
POWER TRIP	71
PUSHING THROUGH	72
RECKLESSNESS	73
FIGHT OR FLIGHT	75

NOT READY	76
MY MOTHER DOESN'T KNOW THAT I STARVE MYSELF	77
DAY BY DAY	78
MERRY CHRISTMAS	79
DRIP	80
CARTOGRAPHER	82
BALLPOINT PENS	83
SUMMER NIGHTS	84
THE GIRL BEFORE	86
DON'T WALK BAREFOOT IN NEW ORLEANS	88
INSURANCE	89
YOU ASKED ME	91
IGNITE	93
GOLD	94
I'LL ALWAYS BE THAT AGE	95
HUNGER PAINS	100
BLACKBIRD	101
CHEMICAL REACTIONS	102
THE DARKEST OF NIGHTS	103
FRENCH TOAST	105
SOME STORIES ARE BETTER LEFT UNTOLD	107
REAL ESTATE	109
YOU CHANGED MY MIND	110
JIGSAW	111
HUNGER	113
HEARTACHE	114
FOREST FIRES	115

- 50M VOLTS 116
- ASSISTED SUICIDE 117
- BLOOD, SWEAT, AND WHATEVER............................ 118
- PIECES.. 120
- COMING TO TERMS... 122
- SHOWER THOUGHTS 124
- POISON NO. 2 125
- REDUCE, REUSE 126
- HOW COULD YOU? 127
- ME, MYSELF, AND I 129
- JUST BREATHE 131
- NO MORE APOLOGIES... 133
- I HATE SUNFLOWERS.. 135
- MINDLESS RANTING 136
- THE GIVING TREE... 138
- HOW COULD YOU? REVISED 142
- THE BLESSING OF FORGETFULNESS 143
- DEAR DAUGHTER,... 144
- FIRSTS 146
- THINGS I FOUND WHILE CLEANING OUT MY ATTIC 147

Acknowledgements

I have to start by thanking my mom and dad, who paved the path to my success with their sacrifices. I could never have done this without your love and support. I also want to thank my siblings, Chase and Marcy, and their families, for pushing me to pursue my dreams. Thanks to everyone on the Legacy Book Press team who helped make my dreams a reality. Thank you for giving me a chance to flourish. To Shannon and Kelsey W., thank you for always having my back and taking the time to have first looks at my work when I wasn't feeling so confident in my writing. Ryley, thank you for carrying me through some of the darkest moments of my life. I couldn't ask for a better best friend. I would also like to thank Grace, who always had the right words to encourage me when I was feeling hopeless. I must also say a special thank you to Carly, Kimmy, Melanie, Robin, Raleigh, and Sarah, who made my high school years amazing despite the obstacles and who inspired me to write with all my heart. Lastly, I'd like to thank Ali Vicknair, a fellow author, who proved to me that we small-town girls can accomplish anything we put our minds to.

flowering out

What happened to the time
When words poured out of me
Like liquid nitrogen;
Cracking open my ribs,
Peeling away the petals of my heart
To unearth a diamond
At its core.
Releasing an explosion of galaxies
And made-up stars,
Fictional constellations
And playtime fire that burned
Brighter than the midday sun.
Brighter than its rays reflected
On our 1997 Chevy windshields
While sweat dripped down our backs
And the hidden moon
Seemed like it would taste
Like a cold glass of water
With a lemony tang,
Coursing through our veins
Like summer streams
Among boiling blood,
Stirring up the heat
Stirring up the passion
Of an infinity of tiny words
Like bee stings
Bubbling to the surface.

someone to blame

Death was a girl,
Maybe early twenties,
Hair light and fried from the sun.
She wore a tattered baseball T
And white-washed ripped jeans
With foggy Coke-bottle glasses
Perched on the bridge of her nose.
Her eyes were yellow under the lenses
Like coffee stains
Or vomit
A cigarette hung lazily
From her dry and cracking lips.
Red lipstick—or maybe blood—stained the filter.
Her skin was like sandpaper,
Same shade of yellow as her eyes.
Maybe the smoke dyed them both.
In her hands she gripped
Paper gowns and
Plastic buckets
For when the bile rose to the surface.
For when her victims spat out the last of their
    sickness.
For when
Time
Stopped.

Death was a greedy bitch.

saying goodbye

Foreign letters fall from my tongue.
Unfamiliar words
And heinous phrases
Taste like sulfur or chalk or maybe those little
    multivitamins my mom gave me as a kid.

I'm possessed by the devil and he's vomiting out a
    sentence I cannot comprehend;
A circumstance I can't accept because—

No
No
No.

It can't end like this.
I can't accept that this
Blood Fate
Belongs to you.

It can't all stop when you've only begun to shine
And you can't just
Die Leave
Me alone when I still have so much left to learn.

Please,
Please,
Don't make me say
He's gone Goodbye
So soon.
Too soon.

reassurance

The Friday before;
Two days before the end;
We were stopped at a gas station.
I was in the backseat.
Mom was inside buying a lottery ticket.
He was in the driver's seat.

I was crying silently to myself.
I had to be the me that everyone needed me to be.
I had to be strong,
Because for the first time in my sixteen years,
He wasn't.

He asked me,
"You know everything is going to be okay,
Right?"
But he didn't look at me.
He didn't turn around.
Maybe it was because he didn't want to see the
    hesitation in my jaw
When I said, "Of course."

Because even though
He was looking to reassure me,
Deep down, he needed to hear it more.
Because even though he had said he'd lived a good
    life,

He wasn't ready to die.
He could feel life slipping
And he was tearing his hands open
Grasping for the line.
He wasn't ready to leave
And he thought maybe this battle really was just in his head.
So when he'd asked,
Maybe he was hoping that I'd see the fear in his eyes
And tell him that it was unwarranted.

That's why he didn't look at me.
He didn't want me to see his lie,
And he didn't want to see mine.
Even if it meant
Leaving me to fight my own battle
All alone.

past tense

It's hard to think that you are not an "are" anymore;
An "is"
An "am"
A "be" anymore.
I caught myself saying
"He likes the rain,"
But you don't.
Not anymore.
You liked the rain
The storm
The thunder and lightning all gurgling in the sky
Setting fire to our galaxy and proving
That the earth is alive.
It's too bad that you're not here to watch it light up.
You're just a "was"
A "were"
A "then"
And now,
Your past has passed
And there are no more
Is's
Tied to your legacy.

that morning was different

Every day without fail,
I'd take you into my arms,
Breathe in your earthy cologne,
Hold together your leathering skin.
Day by day,
Night by night,
I'd watch as my arms grew tighter
And tighter
And tighter
Around your thinning frame
Until they looped back around to me
As you wasted away
To bone.
To flesh.
To nothing—
A stranger.

But that day was different.
I'm not sure what it was
That caused me to turn away.
Maybe I was simply too busy,
Or maybe I knew.
Maybe I couldn't stand the thought
Of not remembering a whole you.
But the fact is
I didn't.
I knew

As soon as the door slammed shut behind me
—*a casket closing*—
I had made a mistake.
I knew
—*last chance*—
That was it.
But I couldn't turn back.
I couldn't bring myself to look.
I now envy Orpheus
Because at the time
I didn't want to turn around.

In my short stride to the car,
In my drive to school,
I had already traveled between Heaven and Earth
    from you.
My legs carried me over mountains—
Swam through oceans—
Climbed over hills—
And my eyes couldn't bare the strain of looking back
At the life I had already given up.

I could only think
About how
When you needed me the most,
I let you down.

And in the end,
The very last time I held you
Was to say goodbye.

while I sat at the bottom of the swimming pool

Things are quieter down here,
More peaceful in a way—
The way the water envelopes you like a blanket,
A watery grave.
In a way, I do feel as if I've been buried at sea.
Perhaps in another life I was tossed from a pirate
    ship,
Bound at my wrists and ankles
Like a traitor to Poseidon himself.
I don't think I screamed as I plummeted down,
For the Sirens were calling my name.
Or maybe I've been sitting here too long,
Watching my hair feather out like spiderwebs,
Collecting bubbles,
Drowning in chlorine,
Moving in slow motion.
Things are nicer down here.
But that's only because no one can hear you scream—
Not that anyone is listening.

wish list

I want a quiet life
Filled with warm Sunday mornings
Like soft piano in a dining hall.

I want fantasy
That twinkles silently
Like the jewels on my mother's boudoir.

I want love,
To love someone so completely and magnificently
That our words are an added benefit.

I want to be safe,
And I want to stop wondering if I'm better off hurt
Because at least the pain keeps me obedient.

But most of all
I want to see another day
And not be disappointed.

I want to wake up
And not wish that I hadn't.

victorian death photography

"Remember you must die."
Victorian England was riddled with death;
Cholera, diphtheria, typhus—
These diseases made death as prevalent as it was trendy.
Even the Queen ushered in a new style of mourning attire.

"Remember you must die."
Death was a statement, a final bow, art even.
Bodies stood up on display to present to the world a morbid curiosity,
An immortal image of mortality itself.
Illness left the bodies immaculately worn.

"Remember you must die."
Eyes would often be painted onto the photo afterwards,
And locks of the corpse's hair would be set aside to keep.
The Victorian people were not afraid of loss,
They prepared for it.

"Remember you will die."
I wasn't prepared.

take a picture

Eyes are quiet when they pour themselves out into
    the world
Like a silent tsunami,
And they take in even more
Like a sponge,
Writhing and expanding,
Filling up with gold and silver.
But even gold is buried
Beneath dirt and soil.
And our eyes take that in too.
They take it all,
All the good
And all the gray.
So as I let your eyes take me in one final time,
I watch
As the universe condenses within your pupils
And dissipates—
Because laughter will always fade to an echo,
And echo to phantom.
And the sun can only hold so much of Heaven
Before it implodes.

selfish

My dream
Was to run
A billion miles away from here,
Abandoning the pain,
Releasing the guilt,
Choosing to forget,
And learning to forgive.
But after you were gone,
I realized my dreams would never come true.
I was selfish then.
Childish.
And it took losing you
To see it.

poison

I am scared that
The touch of my fingertips
To your chest
Will darken your heart
Beyond recognition.

But your eyes are so convincing
When you beg me to stay
And fight away the demons
Together.

holding home

Last night I said
You have nice hands.
I didn't say
They feel like my father's,
Or that
The scar under your knuckle reminds me of the one
    on his palm.
I didn't say
Your hands make me feel safe.
Like turning the key before bed.
I didn't say
They feel like still water—
Like the first break of a calm surface.
And I definitely didn't say
They remind me of home.

it's a process

The process of healing
Is a glutton for time—
As we sit,
And think,
And question
All the things we could be doing
If we weren't so busy
Healing.

familiar

Resemblance is often found in the most unfortunate
 of places.
The familiar bee sting of a flu shot,
The smell of his cologne at the mall,
The cage of hornets in your chest at the peak of a
 rollercoaster—
In my case,
I found familiarity in your voice,
Which so delicately resembles my father's.
I couldn't help but berate myself over the possibility
That my love was actually deep loss
Concealed as passion,
But then you sang,
And my father never sang like you do and—
God I've never wanted to listen to a broken record,
But I could listen to yours for the rest of my life
 and—
You. I still hear you. I still hear your voice in my
 dreams, in my bones.
I said your voice sounds like thunder because I feel it
 rumbling under my skin,
But that's only because I've made you a part of my
 blood.
Tell me where the lightning strikes
And I'll meet you there when you stop singing.
I'll burn you onto my own little disk
And fall asleep to the echo of your syllables—

Every so sweetly crafted—
As if your lips were a locksmith
And my soul is the door you've just opened.
Take everything you can find
Because I would love nothing more
Than to belong to you.
I see familiarity in you,
Because that's where I see my future.

supply and demand

Magic is in short supply these days;
We're all just grasping—
Clinging to the hope
That we can bottle up a shimmer
And turn it into gold.

russian nesting dolls

When I was younger, my grandparents had a television cabinet filled with souvenirs from their worldly expeditions. I remember this because my grandfather always said that he wanted to take me to Norway when I was older. Well I'm older now, and he has cancer.
Anyway.
Among the Celtic folktale book, he'd read to me while I sat upon his lap, and the handmade troll figurines depicting those ugly little creatures holding hands, there was also a little Russian nesting doll. It seemed so out of place now that I think of it. And it wasn't so "little" at the time, or at least in comparison to my toddler hands.
Its red and blue patterns, its small, picturesque face painted on by nimble fingers, its slightly heart-shaped mouth—it seemed like a round little princess compared to the other tiny monsters.
My cousin and I would split her up—take her apart and divide her "children" between the two of us.
We'd try to twist her two wooden halves so that the painted swirls would line up perfectly. But the aging wood would screech with friction.
I remember squishing up my nose and biting my tongue, determined to make both halves connect despite the sharp noise piercing through my eye sockets.

I'm older now, but I still cringe at the memory of that sound. It still echoes in my bones, in my teeth. I'm an adult now, but I still hear the sound of my grandmother reciting recipes in the kitchen while my cousin and I played with those dolls. My grandmother has dementia now.

I'm older now, but my skin still bears the scars from my childhood. One from the time I fell from my grandparents' tree after seeing a dead chicken picked apart by an owl. Another from the time I saw my mother crying after her mom called her a whore. And my knuckle still clicks from the time I broke my finger playing softball. I still have a crick in my neck from when I fell down the stairs while playing hide-and-seek. I don't remember who I was hiding from. But I remember being afraid. Maybe I was running from the ghost that lived in our attic.

Either way, my body still holds those memories. My muscles still hang on to all that pain. And every year, it gets a little heavier. Right when I think it's time to leave those little broken bits of myself behind, another piece of me shatters, and I tear apart my hands while grasping at the shards.

So what happens once it gets too heavy? Sometimes I can feel my bones about to collapse under the pressure, but somehow, I'm still standing. Does that make me strong, or am I just stubborn? Does strength fizzle out, and does stubbornness give in? Will my soul fall apart before my body fails? Which one will go first? It's only a matter of time, I'm sure. So much time has been squeezed into so few years. Did I grow up too fast? Or did the world fall apart at just the wrong time? Did I grow up at all? Is life this heavy for everyone else? Or did I just fall short?

It's time to put the dolls back together.

volunteer work

It got really quiet in the days that followed.
The downpour grew dry,
And that murky cold faded into sunshine.
The doorbell stopped checking in every hour;
Maybe once,
Twice a day if we were lucky.
And then even that stopped.

The consistent traffic
Had worn the mat threadbare,
And the "Welcome" seemed naked.

Too quiet.
Too lonely.
The loss of one person attracted hundreds,
But once the debris was swept away,
The charity ceased.

I guess they didn't realize
That the wood and nails
May be scavenged,
But now there's just an empty lot
Where our home once stood.
And there's nowhere left for us to go.

But good job cleaning up.

bedtime prayer

If I should die before I wake,
I pray the Lord my soul to take,
And fly me up to heavens high,
Where flurries of angels guard the sky;

If I should die before I spoil,
I say plant me with seed and soil,
So that my ashes don't rot and rust,
But bring forth life from settled dust;

But if I shall live to see tomorrow,
I promise I won't wallow in sorrow,
And if I should ever see you again,
I promise you I'll kiss you then.

I am the girl with the rose tattoo

A year after I said goodbye,
Mom and I drove to a little tattoo parlor hidden away uptown.
You had always loved roses,
Though you said not to waste money on flowers for your funeral.
You said we didn't need more things that would die in there.
Yet, roses began showing up.
On our doorstep,
In passing,
In colorful graffiti in the French Quarter.
I smelled roses sometimes, too.
When I'd think of you,
I could almost catch a hint of your cologne.
I guess it was only natural
For us to ink those flowers into our wrists.
I like to think
That perhaps you had held my hand
As the needle left gardens along my skin
Watered with blood,
Fertilized by tears.

I like to think
That this rose on my arm
Is the last you gave to me.
I've learned since then,
That flowers may wither
And the earth may rot,
But some roses
Never die.
I wish you could've been a rose.

new addictions

The moon was drunk
And the stars were high
And the universe was an addict
And I saw it all in your smile
And I became intoxicated.

all the seasons of you

Your lips taste like powdered sugar
On cool winter nights,
Like Christmas cookies
Mixed with the sweetness of syrup and milk.

In summer they taste like a blue-raspberry lollipop
Tucked lazily between my teeth
As I dip my feet into the sun-heated swimming pool
And listen as children laugh and count the seconds
    they can hold their breaths.

The spring leaves traces of pollen
And your lips are coated in honey.
It runs down my throat and fills my mouth with kind
    words,
Intoxicates every memory like a hazy dream of green
    meadows and orange sunsets.

When the leaves flutter to the ground
And autumn finally arrives
You taste like cinnamon and apples and earth,
Like the harvest and hand-knitted blankets next to the
    fireplace.

Every day is another 24 hours of you,
And every year is another lifetime
Spent with your smile
To tell when the seasons change.

cheesy domestic fantasies

A round wooden table
In a tiny log cabin
In the middle of the countryside
Or maybe just in the middle of nowhere special
Overlooking rolling hilltops
Set high above the trickling creeks

Our hands brush against each other
Across an array of strawberries (not quite ripe)
And fresh bread (that we kneaded ourselves)

The room smells of pastry and warmth and cinnamon
And the roses at the centerpiece
Fill the dining room with perfume.

Your fingertips grace my skin absentmindedly
Sending small shocks of hearth up my arm.
I hardly notice it.
But I can almost hear the crackling
Even though we're in the dead of summer.

Even though
We sit in silence,
And let the hours pass
Without a word
Without a care.

her trek

Time is a wanderlust harlot,
Skipping from minute to minute,
Seconds passing by
Without a word,
Without resolve.
No time for goodbyes.
She leaves you
Beaten down,
Violated,
And then she's gone
Before the sun rises,
Before the light shines upon her sins
Demanding reconciliation.
Too little
Too late.
Never enough
Of her body like honey
To satisfy the need
Of forever.

eyes like the ocean

Scratch that.

Rewind.

More like a river
Flowing with joy,
Abundant with life
And love
Filled with the ecosystems
Of families
Who sacrifice the waste
For warmth.

Crashing waves
In anger
Eroding away the bedrock,
Piece by piece,
Pebble by pebble.
Threatening destruction,
Promising apocalypse,
Warning the end.

Sadness like a tsunami
A flurry of insecurities
Bombarding your senses
From every direction
Which way up?

How to get out?
Will this ever end?
Is this it?

Oh
But when he smiles
I see the sunlight
Reflected off the surface
Of the still-as-glass sea;
An explosion of orange
And yellow
And pink
And all the soft hues
That call upon the dawn
After the worst has passed
And the only way to go
Is forward.

bandaids

I've been ripping off bandaids for far too long.
I think my skin has begun to chafe and ache and
    bleed,
When all along
I thought patches would help
And
Keep it inside,
But
The blood still boils
And
The tears still bubble
And
Ripping off bandaids
Simply
Reopens the cut
And
Lets it
F l o w.

Someone
Please
Teach me how to heal
Without saying goodbye.
Because I don't think a bandaid can fix this,
And I don't know how to fix it myself
All alone.
I'm tired of being alone.

lighthouse

The way she looks at you,
Like you're a lighthouse,
Like she's a ship
Lost at sea
Desperately
Searching
For some sign
That she's not stranded
All alone
In the blue
In the waves
In the dark
That her grave won't be the ocean
And her only witness
A lighthouse.

a different kind of magic

When I was no more than seven,
I wanted to be a witch.
All October winds
And rumbling skies.
I wanted the wands
And fairy princesses,
I wanted to feel the electricity in my veins
When I had nature at my command
And when the sun and moon
Deserved my only worship.

Hot summer days
In the backyard of our little townhouse
While my mesh fairy wings
Hung from my shoulders
And the dingy fabric
Of pink costume burlap
Chafed my arms
As I waved a muddy stick in the air
Chanting random words in Cajun French that my dad
    taught me
For the foreign
Held whimsicality
That I interpreted as magic.
So I sang about hats
And sexual innuendos
(Probably)

With wet grass between my toes
And dirt on my sleeve
And I convinced myself that
That was all I needed to cast spells.

My dreams were far more ambitious then.
I yearned
Not to take over the world,
But to control the very laws by which it abides.
To wrap nature around my pinky finger
And share in its motherhood.

Now, I have other dreams.
Dreams of surviving.
Of living on.
Of being remembered.
I used to fear the dark
And the end of a sorcery filled day,
But now I fear abandonment
And everyone forgetting the witch's name
After she's been burned out.

good morning

After I met you,
I would wake up every morning
With your lips pressed against my ear
Whispering the words
"*I love you*"
As lyrically as the lark.
No need to hit snooze.
I realized after a while
That the daylight held promises of your touch,
Your voice,
Your presence;
And because of you
I became a morning person.

party's over

Tell them you feel like fainting.
Then lock yourself up
In a muggy little restroom
To smear red,
Or pink,
Maybe purple
Onto your fading lips.
Crouch in the stall,
Dim where the light doesn't reach,
And hope that
They don't hear you crying—
Or peeing—
Depending on what you drank.

Tell them the world is made of glass,
And that right now
Your feet feel like sledgehammers.
Hide until people stop wondering where you went.
Press your phone to your ear,
And hold a hand over your mouth
To stifle the sobs
As you listen to the voicemail
And wish
You had called him one last time.

Tell them you are tired.
But never tell them that you are sad.
Never tell them that you are broken.
It's nobody's business.

being human

The most difficult part
Is learning to love yourself
When there's a *How To* guide
For being human
With a list of things
You're supposed to hate.

wild nights

Run away with me, Emily!
Show me what wild nights lie beyond the opaque
    covers of my restless slumber—
Give me the luxury of sailing among the breeze
In the break of morning light
Your hand in mine—
Run away with me!
Sing to me the calls of the wild——the calls of the
    ocean——
from within my blood.
When I am with you,
Bring to life those wild nights—
And live wildly with me!

I'm still trying

I try to be the person
That I needed so long ago
When I was young and stupid and naive,
When I was young.
I'm still young though
No matter how long
my feet have trudged this ground
Or how much carbon dioxide
Has been pushed from my lungs,
Because when I was young
I needed someone like me,
But I have yet to grow into the mold that I have set
    for myself.
I have yet to become the strong, courageous,
    compassionate woman
That little girl needed to see in herself.
I'm still a little girl.
I'm still young.
Still stupid.
Still small.

But I'm getting there.

papercuts

I let them carve their signatures
Into my wooden skin
Hardened from the humiliation
And torment
Of the names written on top.
They pick away my branches
One by one
Promise to return with something better
Something knew,
But instead I watch
As the smoke plums
Up
Into the clouds
As they use my flesh as firewood
To bring alive
Their burned-out confidence

or maybe I just think too much

I've been suddenly bombarded
With the impending terror
That there's a possibility
That I'll never amount to anything,

And that everything I've to prove for my work
Will be in vain,
And my memory will be worthless
And just as passing as the wind,

That all my hopes and dreams and ambitions
Are laced with the carnival magic of childhood
    fantasy
And therefore can only ever exist
In my imagination.

the death of venus

Rising from the sea she breathed
Her very first breath of life,
And all the seraphs of the sky
Sang to welcome Vulcan's wife;

She reigned upon the broken world,
Lighting on her thighs,
For the gods so loved her daring gaze,
They carved earth into her eyes;

Her belly rolled with the bellowing waves
From which she had been born,
And no woman nor man alive
Could find within them scorn;

Venus leapt towards the sky,
Touching the bewitched moon,
And from that graze He gifted her
With the craters of stardust runes;

All of Heaven and all of Earth
Cried out to their beckoning queen,
But the goddess simply frowned at them
Knowing that her image would soon be obscene;

As the world aged with feigned grace,
Her wonder left behind,
She watched her daughters primp and poke,
Until butchering the sanctity of mankind;

No flaw uncensored nor inch un-smoothed,
Beauty's children were battered and cut
Until their mother's face diminished,
A heap of plastic beginning to rot;

Venus wept in memory
Of the ballads her angels once sang,
But the only beauty they cared for now
Required humanity's pain;

The world will paint their own Venus,
But this one is out of breath,
For they are willing to waste away
And bring along Venus' death.

april

Scratch out the little box
Of that day
With a fat black marker.

Draw up a void
And let that memory fall
Down
Down
Down
Drowning
In nothingness
Until it dissipates.

Throw out yesterday's sorrow
With this morning's garbage;
Shoving waste from windows
Letting them crash onto the pavement.

Someone else's problem.

Stitch up the gash
With paperclips
And watch as it opens itself back up
Again
And again
And again
Always when you're least expecting it.

Punch a hole in the calendar
And don't patch up the destruction.

Hollow out a place in time
And watch the world take over
To patch up what's missing.

Only time will tell
If that day will resurrect.

excerpt from the only love letter my father ever wrote

"You deserve to be happy."

He underlined each word individually in the chicken-scratch my dad was known for scribbling. Five tally marks, counting up the five words now etched into my heart, into my skin. I wonder if he knew while writing this letter so many years ago, that his daughter would one day use his words as ammunition. I wonder if he knew that this long-dried ink would bubble and burn against my fingertips like poison. I wonder if he knew his words would be mocking me now, telling me false truths upon which to rest my head only to awaken in a bed of nails.
I wonder if he possessed me to find them.
Why else would I have read that letter? I didn't want to. It felt like a dirty little secret reading that letter. The author had been long dead, and the recipient was none the wiser, so how else was I supposed to feel? Maybe that's why his words lacerated my lungs, wrapped barbed wire around my throat. His words weren't meant for me. But I needed them the most.
When I needed him the most—
Well, we all know how that goes.

patience is a virtue

Hold me gently,
And kiss me slowly.

Take your time;
Don't claw
And bite
And hang onto me
Like a rope on board a ship
And, baby,
You're going d
           o
               w
                   n.
Sinking,
Flailing beneath the waves;
Coughing up salt and water and
I love you's
Spat out like venom.

Don't rush
And push
And don't
Cling to me like you're starved;
Like you haven't eaten in days and your stomach is
    growling and saying
Take her,

Because starvation lusts for scraps
And doesn't savor the taste and texture and
It doesn't appreciate the sugary syrup
Dripping from your teeth
As they sink into my lips.

I, your prey, am your relief;
But if you let your fingers
Grace my skin,
Barely touching—

And let your mouth
Draw up maps
Of my face,
Of my body,
Of my soul—

Then I could be your garden,
Giving back to you
Tenfold of what you put into
Caring for me,
Nurturing me,
Showing me—

That this is not by chance,
Or by hunger,
Or by desperation—
But by patience
And by knowing
That what we will harvest
Is worth the sowing,
Worth the wait,
Worth your time.

tired

When sleep has one hand
Gripping your ankles
And pulling you far beneath the surface
And you want to let the weight of the ocean
Meld together your brokenness,
But life has a crane
Clamped around your throat
Thrusting you back into the world
Like a newborn thrust into life,
That's it.
That's the awakening.
Will I awaken?

I told the beetle

There was a beetle in the corner of my room that
    night.
I could see his shadow
Crawling along the edge of the carpet.
Crawling over shoes.
Finally, he stopped
On the floor near my bed
And waited.
Maybe he slept.
Maybe he didn't.
Maybe he simply listened
As I whispered my final goodbyes
One more time.
I told him how I had lost you
And how my heart felt like a stone in my chest
And how our family
Wasn't a family
Anymore.
I told him all our stories.
Stories of Friday night movies in the living room,
Stories of fresh peaches and sugar on our back patio,
Stories of the tears leading up to, and following, the
    killing.
The murder.
Massacre.
So many lives were lost that day,
All gone with the departure

Of a single soul.
I told him goodbye one last time,
And every time after that.
I can't remember if I fell asleep,
But when I next opened my eyes,
The beetle was gone.

hands

I miss you.
I miss your calloused hands,
So similar to mine but bigger and darker,
Wrapped around mine.
That little scar on your index finger,
I forgot which hand it was on—
Right or left
Right or left
Right or
Oh, that's right.
You left.
So it doesn't matter.
I'm not angry.
Well maybe I am.
But not at you.
But maybe a little.
I don't know what I'm feeling and that's why I'm so angry.
why did you have to do this—
why did you have to confuse me?

I miss you but I never want to hurt I never want to
    feel this pain again and if I could go back in time
    and tell my younger self to run right then and
    there I would.
I would.
I would rather run away.
I used to be so strong.
but now I can't recognize myself.
It's your fault.

remember me

When our bodies crumble
And our minds fade
Do you think we can feel
Our souls ache?

Do you think we know
That this breath is the last,
Or die still running
From our tainted pasts?

Do you think we're endowed
With wonders unknown;
Or do we simply waste away,
Our legacy, a headstone?

Do you think we can
Taste,
Or touch,
Or see?

Do you think when it's all over
You'll still remember me?

or maybe he's still gone

I wonder if we cried when God first left,
When He turned away,
Told us we need to grow up
Move out
Learn to change a tire
Build a nation
Fix the plumbing.

I wonder if Adam sobbed,
If Eve trembled
When they said goodbye,
Took their first steps
Without training wheels—
On their own.

It's been so long since then.
We've had our rebellions
We've stepped on toes
Burned bridges.
We've showed Him that
We *can* do it alone,
And *you can't tell me what to do anymore.*
We've moved past our goodbyes.

But then our paper houses came fluttering down
And we're scrambling to pick up the cards before it's
 all lost.
But we still can't swallow our pride
To accept defeat.

Now when He looks down on us from above,
All He sees are toddlers
Stumbling around
Desperately searching
To reconnect,
Like a kid lost in a grocery store,
Even when the mom is just on the next aisle.

Like a baby crying for the bottle in its mouth.

grow with me

You told me that you planted that tree in our front
     yard when I was born
So that every year, it would grow with me
And teach me that life will beat me down and autumn
     will break me, and winter will strip away
     whatever is left
But
Spring is always right around the corner when you
     least expect it—
That's when the flowers bloom.

After you died
I didn't think that they'd bloom again.
How could they—without their spring?
Yet little pink and white buds now form on the
     branches like beads of sweat on my brow when I
     cried for you
This same time
Last year.

or am I being greedy

I want to go searching for magic—

I want to put on my boots
And hike up my sleeves
And pull from the earth something meaningful.

But I think this world is a worn down mine.
I think any diamonds that had once been here are
    long gone.
Now I'm left to polish off coals and pretend they
    sparkle.

I'm tired of looking around
And seeing everyone else decked in jewels—
Stones and beads and rocks glittering along their
    collarbones,
Hanging from their ears,
Ticking away the time.

And all I can do
Is stare at barren walls
Threatening to collapse into its own emptiness,
And reach for hollow pockets
In the life I'm trapped in.

power trip

Oh how tightly
Composed you are;
Yet how easy
It is for my lips
To unravel you.

pushing through

Give me an inch
And open the door
Letting me into all your dark places

I'll bring a match
I'll start the fire
And I'll wait out the night

With you.

recklessness

I don't pause
To send the words
I love you
Or to tell him he has stars in his eyes
And galaxies in his smile—
I don't hesitate
To kiss harder,
Deeper,
To pour my love
Into any vessel that will take it
Anybody that will nurture it—
Because tomorrow,
The sun might not rise
Or my eyes might not open
Or I'll trip over a banana peel and die—
The point is:
I'd rather live second by second
As if I'm writing a million goodbye letters;
Every minute
Squeezing every hour for what it's worth
And sipping its liquor,
Getting drunk on the pain,
Getting high on the pleasure,
Than to waste away
In dust,
In ash,
Only a crater left of my existence,

A distant memory
Of a life spent safely tucked away
And well wasted
With fantasies
Of having nothing more
Than peace and quiet.

fight or flight

He fought the good fight
And endured many battles,
He crawled his way up
From the ruins of matter,

He marched on in victory
And persevered in loss,
But he could never win back
The war it had cost,

Though he fell with victor's honor
All cradled in ash,
We still wept at the battle ahead
And the new trials we had to pass,

But he was no soldier
And neither am I,
But he was willing to fight
And all I want is to fly…

not ready

I wonder if I'll be accepting
On my walk toward death's gate
Knowing that I've done all I could do
Tasted life's nectar
And heard its melody,
Put as much gold into the world
As I took from it.
But I fear I'll walk with aching feet
My head constantly turning back
Brows furrowed
Lips ravished
The reaper's hand on the small of my back
Pushing me along
Feeling my seams throb
As they screech with all my untold stories
Wondering why
I had to go
Before they could be f r e e.

my mother doesn't know that I starve myself

But then again, she never asked.
She doesn't know that I smile when my stomach rumbles and cry after dinner.
She doesn't know that every ounce on the scale is another pound on my heart,
And my heart has been cracking under the pressure.
My mother doesn't know that I am sick.
She doesn't know that this "diet" is a death sentence that I've imposed onto myself
For crimes not yet adjourned but
I know I am guilty.
She doesn't know that I only ever lie to her when I tell her I had lunch.
And worst of all,
She doesn't know that it's become a challenge of mine
To see just how long I can go
Before I wither away.
All I ever wanted was to cave in
To waste away
To nothing,
And to become the void
I once wished to fill.

day by day

I miss you in the memories I have yet to create. I read that once. I don't remember when or by who or why. But I remember thinking about how I often dream about the empty seat right up front at my wedding. The absence of you echoes throughout the church until a union is more akin to the sounds of a funeral. I think of my walk down the aisle, and my arm empty of yours. My arm growing sore with each step I take. Having no one to take me up as their own. I think about one less voice of congratulations when my first child is introduced to the world. Their wide eyes searching for the ghost of a person they'll never have the honor of meeting. I think of all the stories I'll have to tell them of you when the nightmares of monsters getting lost in grocery stores keep them awake. I think of my mother. All alone now. I think of me. Not upholding your promise. I think of a life with you still in it, and I wonder if I'd be any better off. I wonder if I'd be given the chance to take those unmade memories for granted. I wonder if you'd be proud of the soldier I've made out of your little girl. Or maybe you'd be sad that the princess dresses have turned to chain mail and tea parties have turned to wakes. Maybe. But I hope, that wherever you may be, I hope you don't forget. I hope you don't forget to say goodnight.

merry christmas

When I was a little girl,
Nothing could make me happier
Than tearing away the paper
To reveal a new toy—
A new distraction.

I'm older now,
And the gift bags and birthday tags
Don't glitter like they used to.
Maybe I'm too old for magic.
Maybe I'm too young to hope
That Christmas mornings will
Ignite in me the fire of my childhood
When childhood has been long swept away.
And maybe I'm too reluctant to realize
That the morning is a gift in itself.

drip

A faucet left running.
Doors unlocked.
House quiet—except for the drip.

A glass tipped over the edge of the dinner table.
Droplets trickling down the legs
Forming pictures on the tile.

A puddle in the bedroom.
All dried up.
No more dripping from that.

I didn't hear the drop.
I didn't see him fall.
But I was there to clean up the blood.

A glass of water
Now emptied out onto the floor.
I should wipe that up.

The sink now overflowing.
Water turning red as it reaches the scene.
I should turn that off.

I just might drown.
I might sink into the ground.
Who will clean me up?

If I have learned anything,
Baptismal rivers only serve to disguise deadly
 currents.
We just might drown together.

cartographer

I travel the landscape
Of your lips;
Every creek,
Every highland,
Mountain,
Valley,
Plain;
I let my own
Draw up directions
To where your heart
Meets mine
Through our touch;
Your love is like fire,
But your kiss is an ocean
That brings new life
To my desert sands;
But the map of your heart
I have yet to transcribe,
For I'm biding my time
For when the moment is right.

ballpoint pens

Once the ink dried
I couldn't scrub you off of me.
Every single
I love you
And
Meet me by the car
Scratched ever-so-lovingly into the palm of my hand during second period.
We used to write each other novels to read over and over when the lull of the lectures made sludge of our minds.
That ink ran through my veins and flowed through my body like fresh water in a stagnant pool, and your words made me drunk on your touch—
The touch that left doodles and poems right above my knee.
Your words made me shiver as if my blood was freezing hot and the world only felt right when you were the narrator.

Now when I see you, I'm tempted to draw on your wrist—that's where your veins tether themselves to your heart and I can see the deep blue of your blood in contrast of the crystals of your eyes.

But what would I write to you
That you don't already know?

summer nights

"Put your seat back," you said.
"I want to show you the stars."

An eternity ago, I watched your ears redden
As the sunroof revealed only one.
I knew you wanted to present this grand gesture,
Something romantic and wild and beautiful.
Something like offering up the heavens for the sake
    of love.
And I knew you were embarrassed
When the universe ruined your plan.
But that one little star was all I needed.
So we laughed
And teased
About the insignificance of romance on such a grand
    scale.
But you had no idea
That that one little star
Changed my life.
You had no idea how hard I fell——
It felt as if I had been plucked from the sky and
    suddenly, I was falling
      down
          down
    d o w n.
And you were right there, falling with me.
You held my hand

And I counted your fingers,
Caressing the curve of your knuckles
As if admiring the spine of a new book——
>Our book
>Our story
>Our fairytale.

We stared at that star
And spoke to each other through the reflections of
    the glass
And I knew.
I knew
I knew right then and there
That if fate was real,
And if God existed,
And if the stars had any say in the way you giggle
    when you're nervous,
That star was our vow.

"I love you," you said.

And that's when we collided.

the girl before

I don't exactly remember the person I was before I
	lost my father.
Something about the way his voice would never echo
	through our hallway again,
Or his cologne would never restock our shelves—
It broke something in me.
I wish some people had met me before all of that had
	happened.
Then maybe they would be more patient.
Even then, those who had known me didn't like the
	person I had become anyway.
So I guess it doesn't matter.
It's not fair that I have to miss out,
I can kick and scream and throw as many tantrums as
	I want.
He was in the bleachers at my brother and sister's
	graduations;
He was by their sides at their weddings;
He rocked their children to sleep.
He will miss all of that with me.
I will miss out on being a graduate, a bride, a mother.
I will forever be the girl who lost someone all too
	soon.
My boyfriend says it's fine but, oh, how I wish he had
	known me.
I wish he had fallen in love with the girl who loved
	life, loved herself, loved her family.

But all that's left
Is the mangled carnage of what grief left behind.
He picked my bones clean and licked my blood from
 his fingers and oh—
How I wish I could gather those broken pieces and
 scraps of torn flesh and present to him
A girl worthy of love.
But when I try to condense the memories become all
 more vivid—
The blood on the walls
On the floor
On his cheek.
Eyes wide open.
I wish I could become someone worth the time and
 effort, but my grief has made me a monster.
That's the funny thing about grief,
First he makes you cry
And then you never cry again.
First he makes you yearn,
And suddenly that gash in your heart isn't filled but
 it's expanded like a black hole and swallowed you
 up and there's nothing left and
God I'm so sorry. I'm so sorry I can't be that girl
 again.
I'm so sorry.

don't walk barefoot in new orleans

The oven crypt was created in New Orleans in the 1800s in response to the Catholic church's forbiddance of cremation. Before being bought by the United States, the city was run by the French and Spanish. Though France and Spain were both Catholic countries, they had been under Roman control for centuries, therefore adopting Roman traditions of above-ground burial. These tombs would allow for several instances of cremated remains to be buried within the same crypt. But because New Orleans abided by the rules of the Catholic church, they had to find another way to maintain proper burials without an overflow of corpses flooding the streets during hurricane season. This led to the oven crypt, which earned its name because of its eerily similar appearance to a bread oven. You see, after one year and one day, a diseased body was believed to no longer be a threat to the living. So after the allotted time, the oven crypt could be opened up and the remains could be pushed to the back of the chamber. This would allow for multiple people to be buried in a single crypt over time. What does this have to do with walking barefoot in New Orleans?

Do you think the dead wear shoes?

insurance

We like to imagine ourselves,
So many years from now,
Living the lives we've always dreamed of.

Dresses we'll never wear,
Holding hands
With people we'll never meet

Walking down an aisle of blood roses
Two weeks past their expiration.

We like to fantasize
About places we'll never visit
With crystal waters and blue skies,

In the arms of a person we'll never have the chance to
    love
With daring dark eyes that soften
Just for us.

We like to think
That there is more to life than this,
More to life than work,
More to life than pain.
We want to play,
We want to laugh,
We want to live recklessly
And come home to safety.

But for that
We must bare our souls
And empty our pockets
To pay
For all the doubts that prevent it.

you asked me...

"Why do you love me?"
That's an interesting question.
It makes me think about all the little milestones we
    created,
As if puppeteering toy families in a dollhouse
And watching a little world form between us.

I think of our first kiss.
It wasn't magical.
It wasn't perfect or beautiful or even good.
It was sloppy and hesitant and lasted a little too long
    but—
the way you looked at me after—
God.

That smile.
I wasn't scared anymore after that.
Every kiss felt like a new beginning,
And every touch felt like the first gush of air
    conditioning when you open the door after
    playing outside all day on a hot summer
    afternoon.

Every word that fell from your lips became
My bible
My scripture
My lifeline.

Why do I love you?
Who said I had a choice?

ignite

You ignited within my soul
The flame of ten thousand suns,
All expanding and gurgling
With the unbridled rage
Of a looming destruction.

gold

Magic is in short supply these days;
We're all just grasping,
Clinging to the hope
That we can bottle up a shimmer
And spin it into gold.

I'll always be that age

At least that's what they say.

I want to live and breathe and run and *love*—

I want to scream and cry and pierce holes in my skin
    and tally up the scars and give them colors;
And, oh,
I want to love.

I want to love so badly.
Someone,
Something,
Anyone,
Anything,

I want to give myself away
And I want to fall in love with the reflection of myself
    I see in their eyes;
The one that sees the flaws
But paints them anyway
Because they see that beauty is just
A sad imitation of love.

Beauty is an ad reel,
A billboard,
Smooth skin straight teeth
And, no don't cry,

Someone on standby, her mascara's running.

Beauty is flawed and bruised and fucked and I want
    to
Tear
    Myself
        Open
            And
                Bleed.
Red like *Revlon #725*

Beauty is
Stop touching your face
And
Maybe go gluten free?
And
Flaunt what you've got.

But what have I got
Besides back pain
And neck strain
From the constant pressure of
Wear these to make you look taller;

Tell me,
What have I got
Besides red eyes and swollen lips and a stuffy nose
    and an empty belly
And centuries worth of battles—
Soldiers at war

In my heart
In my brain
In my posture—
Would a cookie really kill me?
No, but an extra pound will put me to shame.

Beauty is
Paint your face
But
Not too much;

You look sick
Or
What a fucking slut.

Beauty is a scam—
A fucking nightmare.
Beauty is plastic
And pretend and rotten and disgusting.

But—

Love
Is pain and joy and heartbreak and color and
Did you eat today?
Instead of
Maybe lay off the pizza.

Love is warm,
Sometimes hot,
But never cold and porcelain like the glossy covers of magazines or TV screens or perfect poreless noses.

Love is loud and obnoxious and hilarious and breathtaking and—
Beautiful.

Yes,
Love is true beauty.
We tried to put a price on it,
But just look
And see
At how chipped teeth align
When formed into a smile
From the person who has their heart
Pressed up against yours;

Because you can't fake love
In the same way you can fake perfection.
Because you can't get a *Princess Diary* makeover and be happy.

I'm sure even the princess missed her knee-highs in winter.
I'm sure that *Covergirl* magic can't heal the brokenness inside me.

But love—
Love will make me
g l o w.

hunger pains

I'm hungry for a life
Filled to the brim with
All the things I'm missing now.

Perhaps waiting
Is the nemesis to
Succeeding.

blackbird

I found a bird in the brush the other day,
But he didn't sing.
He croaked with the symphonies swelling in his chest,
But his mouth could not contain his song.

I know I am capable of happiness—
Of light.
But perhaps my soul isn't strong enough.
Perhaps now is not my time.

Or maybe, it's God's cruel joke—
To create a bird that cannot sing;
To birth a soul that cannot shine.

Or maybe it's a back-handed compliment,
To give me the melody
And steal away my voice.

chemical reactions

When you looked at me
I could feel every cell
Reacting to your gaze.

So I turned away,
I hid my face.

I didn't want you to see
The chemicals
Churning in my cheeks.

I didn't want you to see
What you do to me
What you make of me.

I didn't want you to see
How every fiber of my being
Is completely
And utterly
Devoted to you.

Even if you don't love me back.

the darkest of nights

I used to be afraid of the sky.
I thought that if I stared long enough
I'd fall right in.

I thought that the blue above my head
Was just an ocean
Waiting to swallow me whole.

I guess I was scared that
If I let my mind wander to the stars,
I would never get it back.

I guess I was scared
That the idea of nothingness
Would be more appealing than anything keeping me
    grounded.

Oh, how many sunsets I have missed out on
Because I was too afraid to open my eyes.
How many stars have I left uncounted?

But when I met you,
You taught me how to
Count the colors of a sunrise.

Holding onto you,
I didn't mind falling.
I figured the crash would be worth it.

The day you left,
You took the sun with you.
I've only seen the dark since you stole away my light.

But only in the dark
do the brightest of stars shine.
please don't take that away from me too.

french toast

When I was younger, my dad would wake me up early every Saturday morning to make me French toast. This became something of a tradition for us. Growing up, I thought it was just the most amazing thing. Now that I'm older, and now that he's gone, I asked my mom for his recipe. I put a little spin on it though.

First, you'll need a bowl. Any bowl will do. Just something big enough to dip a slice of bread in. Then you need to pick your bread. We've always used the bread that comes from our neighborhood grocery store down the street. I remember many mornings of being stuffed into my father's truck and loaded into the seat of a shopping cart. The white bread was our favorite.

My dad always used two eggs, but I cut it down to one. It makes the toast a little sweeter I think.

About a cup of milk; any kind will work, but I use almond milk now. My dad always preferred 2%, but my mom and I don't really use milk anymore, so it's easier to buy something that'll take longer to spoil. For a special treat, use chocolate milk.

After your eggs and milk are whisked together, it's time to add your cinnamon and vanilla. Now the cinnamon is what makes the French toast crispy on the outside if you do it right. The best way to accomplish this is to add extra cinnamon to each side of the bread once it's cooking on the pan. It'll look a little burnt, but that's how you know you're doing it right.

Now don't cook it for too long—you want the inside to be gooey.

Once you're done, it's time to decorate. I like to add blackberries that I picked from my grandpa's backyard. When I was little, my dad would pour syrup and copious amount of powdered sugar on top. My sweet tooth isn't as strong as it used to be, though.

And that's it. Enjoy your Saturday morning. You never know how many lazy weekends you have left.

some stories are better left untold

I don't want to write about heartbreak while my heart
    is broken.
I can't drown out the sound of glass shattering with
    the click of my keyboard.
I can't numb the ache in my belly with the honey of
    my words.
Words aren't powerful.
They don't fix anything.
Words are just fairytales, storybooks, fiction.
If my words can't help me now
Then what's the point?
If I can't make narrow the gap between us
With my ladder of paragraphs,
Then why even open my mouth?

I wrote you a letter.
Four days after.
Five minutes before I saw you.
I wrote you a letter
Telling you all the heaviness in my heart.
All the apologies, all the regrets.
I wrote you a novel
Begging you to give me another chance,
To not let my sickness
Make waste of who we are.

You never read my letter.
You burned my novel.
You took two steps back and I realized that my words
 don't mean anything.
Words won't help if you won't listen.

How can I make you listen?

real estate

To love someone
Is to gift them a piece of your heart;
To be in love
Is to let them reside there,
Be the reason for its beating;

And if that love is broken,
That piece in which it was invested
Dies
And leaves the burden of a rotten limb
Throbbing in your chest.

you changed my mind

I had come to accept that fantasy was a myth and that
	love in storybooks was just a caricature of our
	deeply neglected desires for companionship.
I used to read about people falling in love, unable to
	look away, memorizing every scar every freckle
	every inch.
I used to believe in that kind of love.
That crazy, determined, selfless, doting kind of love.
Then I didn't.
I grew up and learned that an author can only write
	from one side and one dream and one hope and
	one desperate plea that sex is not the climax of
	human connection.
And then, I met you.
And I believed again.

But now I'm not so sure.

jigsaw

I guess
In a perfect world,
We are a perfect match.
But I'm still trying to figure out
How we fit
Right here, right now.

My puzzle piece is torn.
It's been through hell
And it's survived to tell the tale.
I'm not sure how.

It was, at one point, as pristine as yours
From when it had left the factory,
Brand new box,
Seal still untampered.

But now my piece is scratched,
Ripped,
Frayed,
Ruined.

And then here you come along,
Still glossy and new.
Your image not yet faded, and you saw familiarity in me.
And we matched.
Somewhat, I guess;
But enough.
Well enough.

But in order to align ourselves,
You had to tear away parts of you
To match my brokenness.
It was the only way to stay together,
The only way to be complete.

You became just as broken as I was,
But I gave you everything I had left.
Still,
It wasn't enough to complete the picture.

But you were so relieved to finally find a comfortable fit
That you tended to old wounds, and tore up new
And accepted them as circumstance;
Even if you were losing yourself,
Piece by piece.

hunger

"Just a taste?"
They beg
And then devour you whole
Leaving nothing but crumbs
From the last of your charred soul.

heartache

Her heart was so full
That it ached in her chest,
So she gave some away
To every stranger she met.

But as time ticked on,
And strangers went away,
She soon realized that
No one would ever stay.

So she bottled up her heart,
And cast aside her ache,
And let the brewing boil,
And awaited what it would make.

forest fires

I thought I saw a home
In the reflection of your eyes.
I thought you mirrored the life from before—
The life I had lost.

I thought—or maybe I simply hoped—
That these kaleidoscopes would omit the fires that set
    my aching hands ablaze.
But here we are now,
Watching our world burn.

50m volts

I used to feel the power
Coursing through my veins
Making my fingertips tingle with every
"I love you."
But not all happiness is magic,
And not all magic is good.

Every "I love you,"
That electricity,
It drained me.
A curse upon myself
Which made me lose myself
To you.

But maybe there's still hope.
I still want to believe in magic.

assisted suicide

I saw you kill yourself last night.
You tied the noose,
Looped it around the post
And stepped off.
I saw the image of the boy I knew
Die.
Just a word.
A bullet in your skull and then
A smile.
Because you didn't realize you were bleeding.
You didn't realize I was watching a suicide.
I etched your obituary into my arms that night.
Scratched with my fingernail
Bright red tally marks
Counting up the tears I saw
Glittering in your eyes
Or maybe they were my own,
Though we both know a laugh
Often hides much more.

blood, sweat, and whatever

The worst part about crying isn't the stuffy nose or swollen lips or double chin.
It's the itchy eyes.
Because when your eyes itch you can't see and when you can't see you can't focus and when you can't focus you think more and when you think more you cry—
I cannot preach that it gets better, because even as I write this I'm still waiting for some kind of sign, some hint of what to do that'll prove I am capable of happiness.
I keep clawing at my eyes
hoping
praying
pleading for him to come back
begging for him to listen.
My eyes feel like mosquito bites and my eyelashes feel like needles and my mouth is tired, but I can't
stop
screaming.

My eyes burn and I want to scratch them out, but I
> got a manicure yesterday and I don't want to
> waste the polish

his favorite color
my favorite shade of pink.

please don't leave
please don't give up on me—
not yet.

pieces

You told me that
Broken
=
Beautiful.
You told me that
My brokenness
Made you
Fall.
But all these scars
Are not appealing.
They are not cosmetic
Or aesthetically pleasing.
I worked hard
To cover them up
To make them heal
To put myself back together.
My pain made me weak
And I was beautiful
Like a daisy
Soft and temporary.

But if I healed
I could be a rose
With thorns to protect me.
Maybe you thought you could be my thorns.
Maybe I thought so too.
But I need to learn
How to fend for myself
If I ever want to fix
Those broken pieces.

coming to terms

I'd be lying if I said I didn't hope every text I receive
 was from you,
Even though I know your words might chip away the
 remainder of my heart which I give so willingly
 to you.
Even though I know I'll be left to die.
I'll break.
I can't help but hope.
I can't help but pray that you'll give the thought of me
 three seconds of your time.
I can't help but replay every moment in which you
 promised me the sun,
only to leave me now in darkness.
I'd be lying if I said I wouldn't come crawling back at
 the snap of your fingers,
the click of your jaw outlining my name.
I said I wouldn't wait for you, but we both know my
 life has been at a stand-still since you left.
You tore me to shreds,
but baby, I'd let you sew me back up if you wanted to.
You broke me,
and I'd do it all over again.
I hope that one day my skin won't ache for the
 electricity in your touch.
I hope that my nights won't be tainted with dreams of
 you.

One day, you'll remember the way my eyes lit up like streetlights the first time you told me you loved me.

One day you'll think about how the girl you broke was the girl who would've given anything just to be yours.

But by then, it may be too late.

shower thoughts

I turn the nozzle
And heat up the water
And let it cascade down my back.
But even as my skin blisters
I still shiver.
A fire couldn't replace
The warmth wrapped up in your arms.

poison no. 2

You're the kind of poison
I drip into my morning coffee,
Savoring the sting
And ignoring the burn
As it seers a hole
In my heart.

reduce, reuse

You used to be
Mt favorite way
To waste time.

how could you?

I hate this. I hate the way you made me feel important, just to take it away. I hate how you painted this future for us, and then slashed through the canvas. I hate how you made me feel worthy, and then you threw me aside. I hate the way you let me trust you, just to turn around and leave the very next day. It took so long for me to give that part of myself to you. It took so long for me to rationalize your intention to remain a part of my life, even throughout my faults. And once I finally made a home for you deep within my heart, you moved out, leaving me vacant. I hate how deeply I rely on you for happiness because you don't rely on me. I hate how every song, every joke, every picture reminds me of you. And I hate that all those perfect moments are tainted with the everlasting sting of heartbreak. I hate that I threw myself away to become yours. But most of all, I hate myself, for not hating you. I want to scream and cry and shake you and rip you apart like you tore open my skin and watched me bleed gold ichor. But I can't. Because I love you. I'll always love you. I'll always find joy in the way you squint your left eye when you smile. And I'll always find sadness in your crooked grin when you are trying not to cry. And I know that this is because you are not evil. You are not cruel. The circumstances thrusted upon us are vile and despicable and unusual but so, so necessary. As much as I hate to admit it. I didn't deserve you. I still don't. But I will. I will fight. Because you are good and kind and vibrant like the warm sunset hues reflecting off the ocean. You are confused and scared and worried that I cannot be helped. You think you are doing what's best for me. But I am sick and tired of people telling me what's best for me. I can take care of myself. I think. I'm sick of the nurses and counselors and social workers telling me to act a certain way, telling me to think a certain way, all because they don't care enough to learn the truth about me. I thought you knew me better than that. I thought I could trust you. I still want to trust you. I want to trust that you have our best interests at heart, but I don't believe in fairytales. "Meant to be" can only go so far; you have to fight for what makes you happy. Maybe you thought it should all come easy. But I'm ready to weather the storm with you for however long it takes, because I know the sunlight after the hurricane is even more iridescent. Don't you miss that?

me, myself, and I

I hope when you see the sky, you still think of me.
I hope the stars always remind you of that night.
I hope every sunset brings back the urge to tell me to
 look outside.
I hope what we had was strong enough to leave an
 imprint on the heavens.

You once told me that I was a baptism.
That I had left a mark on your soul.
That I could never be replaced or erased.

You said that the world is only as colorful
As we paint it.
And you insisted that I was your palette.

So tell me why, my love,
Why did you break me?

I gave you the gun
I just never thought that you'd pull the trigger.

I never thought you'd find joy in my pain
or pleasure in my confusion.

I gave you everything.
I gave you all of me.
I chipped away parts of myself and tied them up with
    a little red bow and a tag that said *Drink me*
And I thought that if I drowned you in my love then
    you'd never want to walk away.

I let you mine away my diamonds.
Now I don't remember how to shine.

Is that why I feel so empty?
I don't know if emptiness is the right word for this.
I keep trying to convince myself that you've damaged
    me beyond forgiveness.
But we both know how my will melts at the comfort
    in your embrace.

I pray that I will be secure enough in my own accord
and strong enough to tell you no
the next time you decide you've missed my company,
The next time you decide that I'm worth a second of
    your time,
The next time you need me to pick you back up.

I pray that I am happy.
I plead that when the time comes,
My first and foremost objective will be to create joy
    for myself instead of looking for it in someone
    else.

just breathe

I see how people get addicted to this.
This feeling.
Weightlessness.
Bliss.

Like you're in the mosh pit but you're wearing
    headphones.
Like the world is a sea and you're stuck in a current.

Adrenaline and serenity
Make an odd couple.
And yet,
They complement each other so amusingly.

I used to be afraid of drowning,
But darling,
to drown with you.
That's the best way to die.

Honey, I'm sure you meant well
But baby, I've got to grow.

You were my bliss,
but perhaps you were not my shelter.

I thought you were an angel,
but angels make mistakes too.
Lucifer himself was once God's favorite.

But your once heavenly reassurance
now turned sour--
baby, I can't help but miss my angel.

Even if you were lying.
Even if you were lying.

I'll always have fond memories of my angel.
But for now, I'll have to accept the rejection of a
 demon
wearing my beloved's crooked smile.

I fell for the ocean in your eyes,
But I don't want to drown anymore.
Don't pull me under again
unless you're prepared to kill me.

no more apologies

The night my dad died,
I kept saying sorry.
I held his bloodied gray hand,
tears flowing onto his tattered shirt;
I bottled up that pain and labeled it as guilt.
Guilt for not being there.
Guilt for it not being me.
It couldn't have been me,
No matter how much I wanted it to be.
I couldn't accept his fate as my own.
I couldn't accept his fate at all.

The night you left me,
I kept saying sorry.
I told you that it was my fault,
and you quietly agreed.
I begged for one more chance.
I pleaded with you not to abandon me before I got
　　better.
You left anyway.
In three months, you replaced me.
And I apologized for not being the girl you wanted
　　me to be.
I accepted the guilt of being too broken to be yours.

The night I stared at the little blue pills,
I kept saying sorry.
When did I forget
How to keep myself afloat in this flood?
Was I not present to board the arc?
If I was guilty,
Who would be my judge?
Who would prosecute me for the sins that I have
    unburdened from others' souls?
Who would be kind enough
To grant me the delicate captivity of punishment
when I felt as untamed as a tortured animal?

Who would say sorry to my mother
And take responsibility for the murder of her child?

I hate sunflowers

You ruined them for me.
I hope I ruined things for you too.

mindless ranting

I'm starting to think that I'm the problem. I try so hard to give and give and give but it makes me resentful once I'm all out of virtues to give. I break, and once I break, they leave. Everyone is bound to leave. He left because I wasn't good enough to work for. She left because I wasn't good enough to wait for. Once they squeezed every last drop of ichor from my veins, they left me to dry out in the sun like a raisin. I often think of my soul as a bare skeleton half-buried in the desert. They use me until my hands are raw and my feet ache and my voice is hoarse. They use me until I'm all used up. My knees are shaking and my nose bleeds and every time I hear your voice, I feel like I'm falling. But not in the lovely way. I've slipped on your broken promises and my face is about to hit the concrete. And no one is there to hear me scream. I feel like I'm behind glass. All strung up like an exhibit. I feel like I am the problem. I feel like a rose, but not in the beautiful way. I feel like people pluck away petals and then toss out my stem for good luck and, God, I feel like a rat caught in a trap lashing out in fear and anger and I keep biting down on fingers but I can't seem to see their faces.

Where did things go so wrong? When did I lose myself? I feel like I have nothing left to give. Like I'm obsolete. I feel like I'm empty. I feel full of pain like I haven't eaten in three days. Why is it that I only feel beautiful when I am hungry?

Why did I do that? Why am I so stupid, shit, why can't I stop crying?
Why did you leave?
Why can't I ever give enough to make you stay?

the giving tree

She wears it well—
The scar you left on her heart.
And I wear it well, too—
Your names etched into my skin.

You were children,
But so was I
When you grazed my hardened flesh with your razor,
Spelling out your promise, your vow
To love her for as long as my hollowing trunk could withstand
The years of having you branded into my side.

You told her that the world will learn
How to accept all your forevers and all your childish I love yous and—
Dammit, I was rooting for you.

You whispered empty promises under the shade of my branches,
Thinking that the space under my willow was a universe in itself
Unable to be brought out into the daylight.

But she took your words and all your smiles and all
 your wishes
And she set them out to dry up like pressed flowers in
 the sun and—
I thought you'd make it.
Dammit, you made me believe in love.

I was so young when I first met you and I didn't
 realize
That the glittering of your eyes
Was just a reflection from the snarl of your bared
 teeth and—
She trusted you.

I held your promises like a time capsule;
I wore your vow like a sash,
And, oh, how I hoped your absence meant that you
 were finally free—
Free to bask in the glory of day and free to me speak
 my proud scar as scripture.

But when I saw her again,
I knew I had been wrong.
Her face was well worn with the sorrows of your
 betrayal—
Her eyes glistened like the bright red polish of a party
 clown's shoe
And she knew she had been duped.

She finally realized that your eyes may have been oceans
But she was drowning.
She was suffocating under the weight of your apologies
But it was a death she welcomed with her kind and knowing ignorance and—
I hate you.

I hate that even as her tears water my soil,
She still cries out for you to return.
I hate that you carved love into the very bones of the earth
Just to set it all ablaze and—

My, how I love you
For the bright pinks and yellows your fire painted before my eyes
In my world of dark green.
But in the wake of your manufactured sunset,
My nature was just as black as your intentions.

I hate you so much because I see how your soul rots
But she still loves you.
She's addicted to the sting of your betrayal
In the same way I grew fond of the pain of my scar.

You may have forgotten about the melody of her
    laugh
But I will never forget your secrets spilled in the dead
    of night.
I was once your haven, remember?
I hold the two of you—
Forever young, forever in love—
Encased in the sanctity of nature's endurance.

Maybe that's why I still smile
As the girl you broke
Traces the wound in my skin
One last time.

Maybe that's why
We still have hope.

how could you? revised

I get it now. I know why you did what you did. You said it was because of me. Because my heart was too heavy to hold, and you could no longer withstand the weight. I know that that's not true. I know why you did it. You did it because you're weak. You couldn't stand the thought of me flowering out of your emotional chokehold. For so long, I stayed pinned beneath your thumb, thinking that the light at the end of the tunnel was you, when really it was the freedom that came with losing you. Flowers need water to grow, but you were more like a hurricane. You drowned me, covered me up, hid me away. You kept me a sprout, when all I wanted was to blossom. I know you still think of me. I know you miss the way I'd look to you like a sunflower looks up to the sun. But I'm not your flower anymore. I am my own. I've grown thorns, and now you can't touch me. Your hands will never again taint my impressionable stem. I thought I loved you, in the same way a dog remains loyal to its abusive owner. But now I am stronger than that. I have bloomed. You can't keep me hidden in your shadow anymore.
Thank you. Thank you for setting me free.

the blessing of forgetfulness

I'm starting to forget the little things,
Like the way my name sounded on your lips.

When your face appears in my dreams at night,
It's blurry,
Like I can't quite remember the curve of your jawline
    like I once did
Or the exact shade of blue in your eyes.

What a gift—
How invigorating—
To finally see that my mind is starting to lose its grip
    on you.

You no longer plague my thoughts
Or interrupt my daydreams.

I can breathe again
Without remembering your breath on my neck,
On my skin.

You're just a whisper,
An echo of a memory I once had.
And even that will disappear too.

dear daughter,

If you're reading this, we made it.
I know the pain you feel.
I'm familiar with the hollow sting of heartbreak and betrayal. I once told your grandma that it was her fault. That I had never asked to be born, so she had pushed this life on me. A life of punishment. I vowed to never subject another soul to the hell in which I was trapped. So if you're reading this, I know your pain.
But if you are alive, dear daughter, that means I found something in this world worth living for. I wouldn't have been selfish enough to force this prison of a life on you if I wasn't positive of the rewards.
Dear daughter, you have fire in your veins.
It's only natural to feel like you're burning up at times. But one day you'll see how the warmth within your heart was actually protecting you from a life of indifference. A life of acceptance. It's a cold cruel world and so little hearth is found at the center.
Dear daughter, do not accept peace. Be the peace. Be the change.
You were brought into this world by love and pain and determination. You were forged by the very flames that assured Moses of God's will. That burning bush, a furnace within your soul. Scream your jurisdictions out into the mess of this earth with confidence. Your words can cause hurricanes and rebuild ecosystems alike. Your tears are capable of flooding a barren

desert.

Sweet girl, please don't forget that you are the perfect culmination of all the women who came before you. You are a warrior unto herself. You are a goddess among those who have never experienced the vibrance of heartache.

You are radiant, dear daughter. You are worthy. And if you ever find yourself wondering what it's all for, I hope you can show this to your daughter someday.

firsts

I didn't have my first peanut butter and jelly sandwich until I was seventeen years old. This wasn't because I had a crappy childhood or anything like that. I had a great childhood. It just never occurred to me before.

When I was ten, I had my first slumber party. Three of my girlfriends came, one being my cousin. I'm not friends with them anymore. Well, except for my cousin. We made red velvet cupcakes and watched Barbie movies.

I rode my first "big girl" rollercoaster when I was thirteen. Up until then, the thought of being held upside-down by a single nylon seatbelt made me want to vomit.

When I was sixteen, I fell in love with a boy before falling in love with myself. He was the first person to lie to me through a smile. Things didn't end well.

I learned how to ride a bike when I was six. My dad and I would go up and down the street playing "eye-spy."

When I was eighteen, I had my first reset.

things I found while cleaning out my attic

1. Yellow baby blanket
2. Dad's old winter jacket
3. My sister's old prom dress
4. A few of my journals from when I first learned to write
5. Pictures of family members who are long gone
6. Pieces of shattered homemade Christmas ornaments
7. Pink sneakers, women's size 8
8. A time capsule filled with newspapers from 2002
9. My brother's senior yearbook
10. A love letter from my dad to my mom
11. Maps my mom used to drive to Louisiana
12. Pictures of my mom's ex-boyfriends
13. Pictures of my ex-boyfriend
14. A stuffed rabbit with a rotted voice box
15. My baby footprints
16. A statue of the Roman goddess Venus
17. Cassette tapes of my dad's first wife
18. A toy tiara

19. Two glass candlestick holders
20. A box of stale bubblegum
21. A photo album from my mom's first wedding
22. A daybed cover
23. A puzzle of Venice, Italy
24. My first kid's bike
25. A Mardi Gras scarf
26. My father's paintings
27. A box of colored pencils

ABOUT THE AUTHOR

Kelsey Villeret was born right on the outskirts of New Orleans, Louisiana. She is 18 years old and has been writing since she was a child. Her work has been featured in school literary magazines, as well as online. She is currently a student at Louisiana State University studying English with a concentration in creative writing.

www.ingramcontent.com/pod-product-compliance
Lightning Source LLC
Chambersburg PA
CBHW030231100526
44583CB00013BA/875